This book is dedicated to the tens of
millions of energetic youth whose
participation is vital to the future
prosperity of the United States of America.

One Day, I Will VOTE!

WRITTEN AND ILLUSTRATED BY

GARRETT WILLIAMS

WWW.ONEDAYIWILLVOTE.COM

GARRETT@ONEDAYIWILLVOTE.COM

WE VOTE WITH OUR VOICE

AND WE VOTE WITH OUR HANDS.

ON RAINY DAYS WE STAY INSIDE.

OUR CLASSROOM MUST DECIDE.

Voting is my superpower.
I will stand tall like a tower.

I am smart and proud.

My voice will be loud.

I LOOK FORWARD TO THE DAY

THAT I'LL VOTE AND HAVE MY SAY.

I CHERISH OUR DEMOCRACY.

FOR SOME, IT'S JUST A FANTASY.

IN ALL THINGS, WE HAVE A CHOICE.

AND FOR THAT, I REJOICE.

One day, I will vote.

Hop on my boat!

EVERY FOUR YEARS WE GET TO VOTE.

DONT FORGET TO WEAR YOUR COAT.

IT'S THE FIRST TUESDAY IN NOVEMBER.

SO IT'S EASY TO REMEMBER.

Not all countries get to vote.

So remember this quote:

"Someone struggled for your right to vote.

Use it."

-Susan B. Anthony

Let me tell you about our glorious flag.

Get ready, I'm about to brag.

The flag is a symbol of our freedom.

Our land is our kingdom.

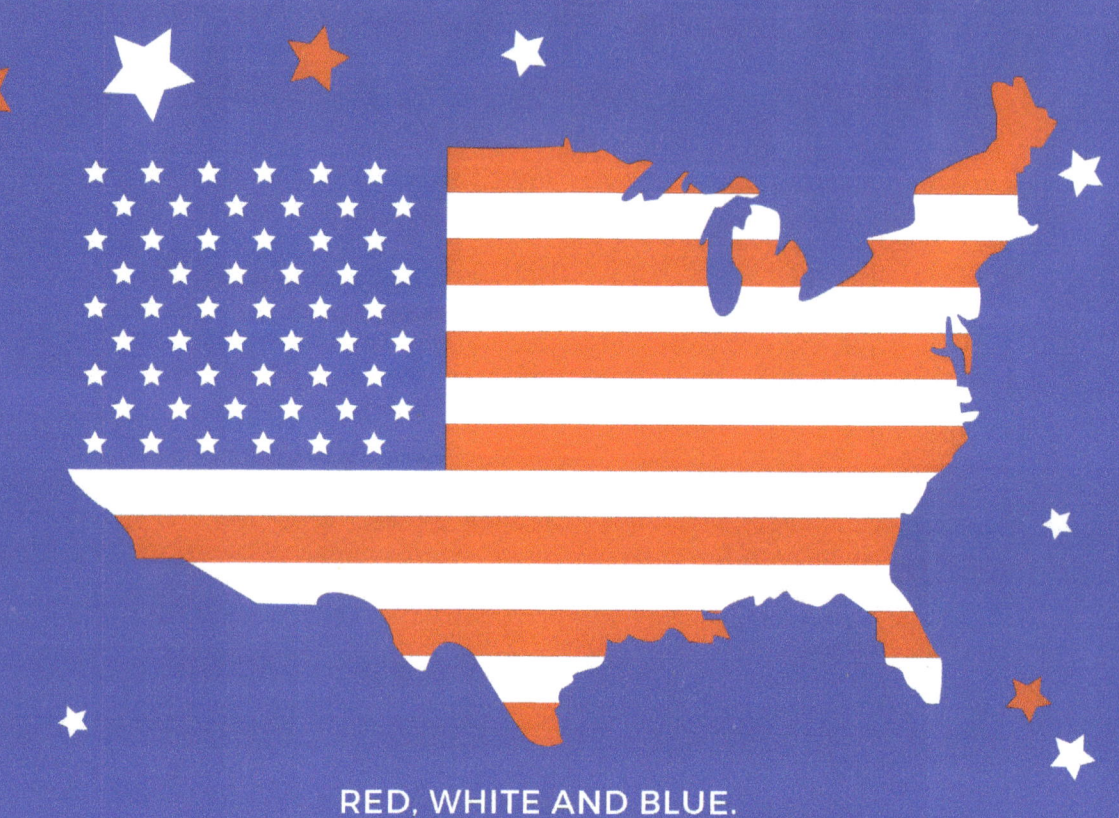

RED, WHITE AND BLUE.

WITH FIFTY WHITE STARS, IT'S TRUE.

EACH STAR REPRESENTS A STATE.

THERE'S MORE, JUST WAIT!

SEVEN RED AND SIX WHITE STRIPES.

THE AMERICAN FLAG IS GLORIOUS IN LIGHTS.

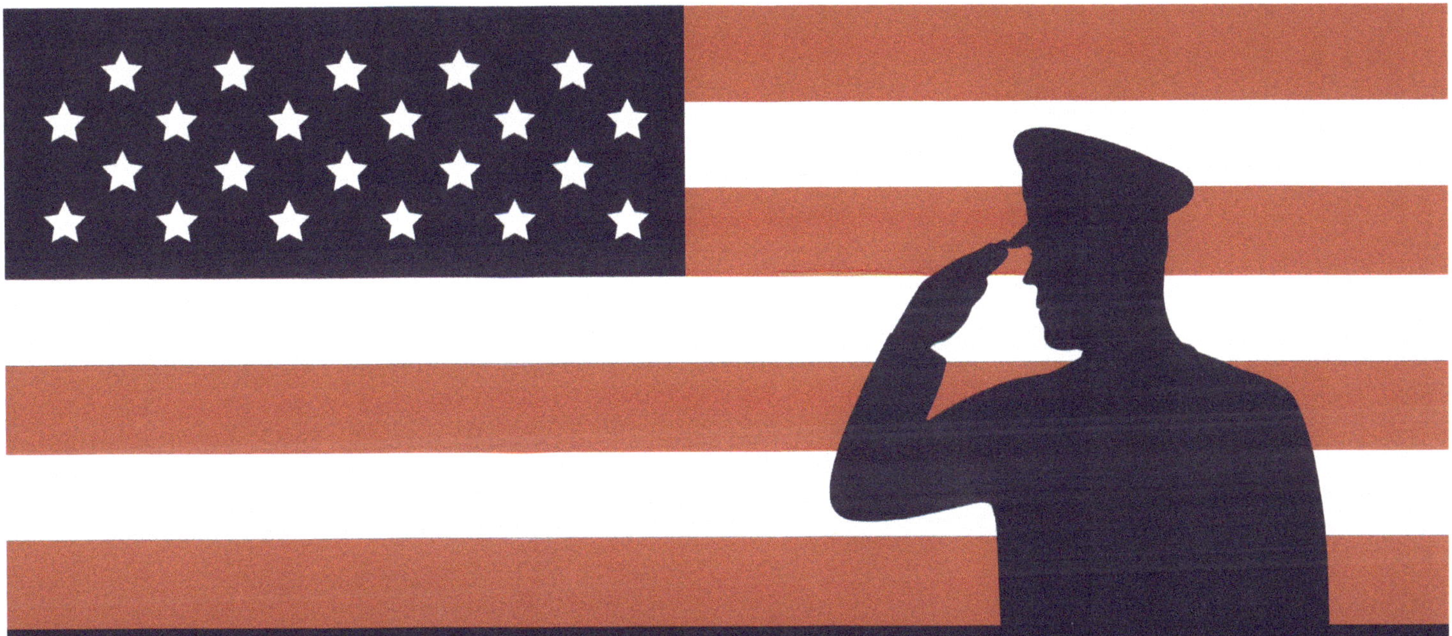

WHO CAN I THANK FOR OUR FREEDOM?

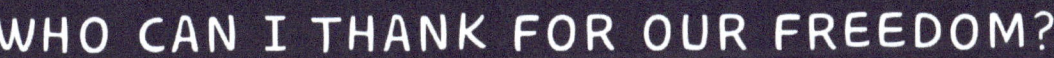

OUR SOLIDERS ARE THE HERO'S.

WE NEED EM!

GIVE US THE VOTE!
VOTES FOR WOMEN
GIVE US THE VOTE NOW
Mr. President How long must women wait for LIBERTY?
VOTES FOR WOMEN

To the women in nineteen twenty.

You did more than plenty.

The Women's Right to Vote.

You rocked the boat!

IN 1870, PROGRESS WAS MADE.

THE MUSIC TRIUMPHANTLY PLAYED.

FINALLY, AFRICAN AMERICAN MEN HAD THE RIGHT TO VOTE.

WHAT A BEAUTIFUL NOTE!

THE DAY WILL COME WHEN I TURN EIGHTEEN.

WHAT A LOVELY SCENE.

Ballots will be counted.

Curiosity is mounted.

Who will our President be?

It might just be me!

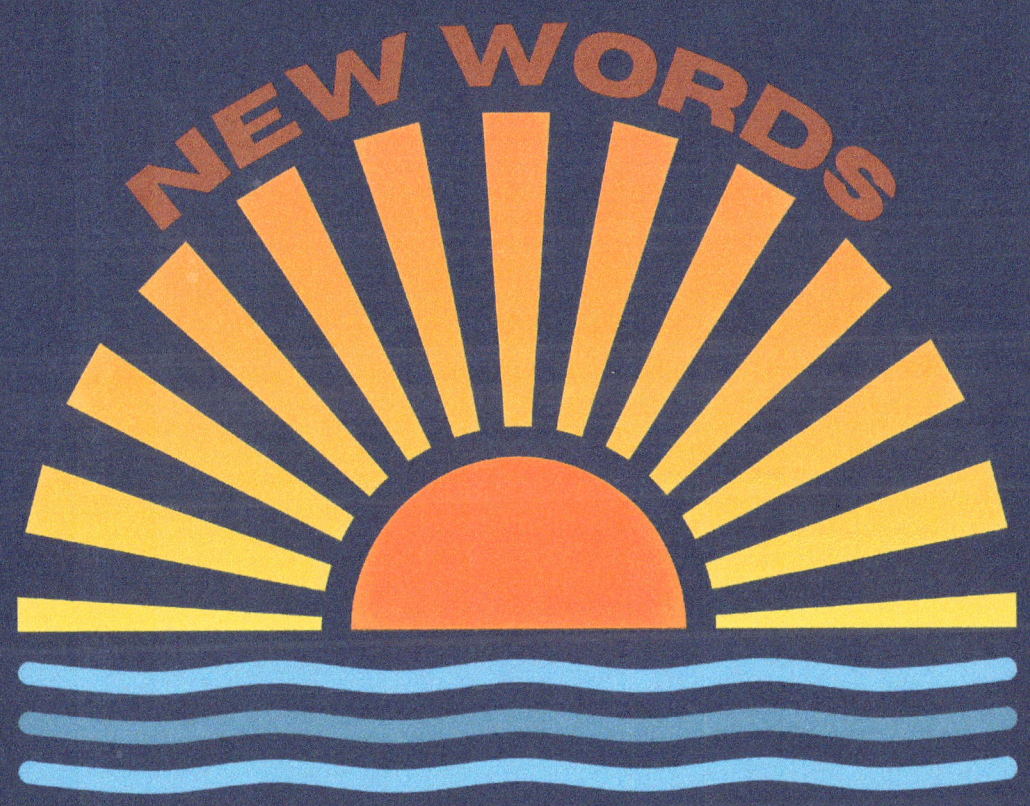

Vocabulary knowledge

Democracy

Ballot

Election

Voting rights

Campaign

Liberty Bell

<u>Democracy</u> is when people choose their leaders by voting. Giving everyone a voice.

<u>Ballot</u> is a form where you choose who you want chosen, or what decisions you want to make.

<u>Election</u> is when people come together to vote and choose their leader or make an important decision.

<u>Voting Rights</u> are rules that make sure everyone has a fair say while voting.

<u>Campaign</u> is when someone who wants to be your future leader goes and shares their ideas and sharing why they're a good fit.

<u>Liberty Bell</u> is a very old bell in the USA that stands for freedom. The Liberty Bell is seen all across the world as a symbol of America's liberty and independence.

Talking points

When can you vote?

At what age can you preregister to vote?

Who is your state Governor?

Who is your Congressperson?

Who are your Senators?

Printed in the USA
CPSIA information can be obtained
at www.ICGtesting.com
LVHW070307051024
792213LV00027B/59